The **Essential** Buyer's Guide

DE LOREAN
DMC-12
1981 to 1983

Your marque expert:
Chris Williams

VELOCE PUBLISHING
THE PUBLISHER OF FINE AUTOMOTIVE BOOKS

www.veloce.co.uk

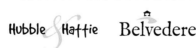

First published in March 2018 by Veloce Publishing Limited, Veloce House, Parkway Farm Business Park, Middle Farm Way,
Poundbury, Dorchester, Dorset, DT1 3AR, England.
Telephone 01305 260068/Fax 01305 250479/email info@veloce.co.uk/web www.veloce.co.uk or www.velocebooks.com.
ISBN: 978-1-787112-32-2 UPC: 6-36847-01232-8.

British Library Cataloguing in Publication Data – A catalogue record for this book is available from the British Library.
Typesetting, design and page make-up all by Veloce Publishing Ltd on Apple Mac.
Printed and bound in India by Replika Press.

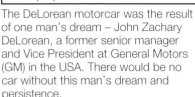

The DeLorean motorcar was the result of one man's dream – John Zachary DeLorean, a former senior manager and Vice President at General Motors (GM) in the USA. There would be no car without this man's dream and persistence.

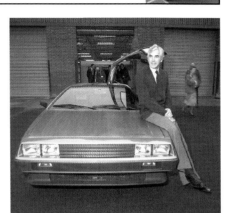

The first cars rolled off the production line in Dunmurry, Belfast, in January 1981, with the last ones being finished off during receivership, in 1983.

When asked for advice on which DeLorean to buy, my answer has always been, "A DeLorean is a DeLorean, is a DeLorean." There were a few minor changes and minor styling tweaks along the way, but there is really only one DeLorean model,

John Zachary DeLorean sitting on VIN 502 outside the factory in January 1981.

sometimes referred to as the DMC-12. The original buyer faced only two choices; three-speed automatic or five-speed manual. Later on there was a choice of interior colour: alongside the original black, you could opt for grey.

In total about 9000 cars were produced, mainly for the American market, almost all in LHD form. 17 were converted to RHDs for and by the factory. There are also a few unusual ones, including three gold-plated and prototype turbo-charged cars, along with several Lotus-built 'Pilot' cars (pre-production models).

All DeLoreans are built on a Lotus-designed backbone chassis/frame. A strong VARI (vacuum-assisted resin injection) underbody is bolted to the epoxy-coated, mild steel chassis, with stainless steel gullwing doors, and body panels bolted onto the underbody. All were fitted with the 2.85-litre PRV (Peugeot Renault Volvo) V6 engine, using a Bosch K-Jetronic fuel-injection system and either a five-speed manual or three-speed automatic gearbox, both supplied by Renault. They had all-round Lockheed/Girling disc brakes, fully independent suspension, also designed by Lotus, energy absorbing front and rear bumpers, space-saver spare wheel, and tool kits.

Throughout this book the 'left' and 'right' sides of the car are always referred to as if seated in the driving seat.

Thanks

My sincere thanks go to the many owners and enthusiasts I have met over the years both at car shows/club meets and online. I would like to thank the many contributors to this book, especially the DeLorean Owners' Club (UK) Historian, Chris Parnham, who has helped with fact checking, supplying pictures and specific advice. Both Chris Parnham and Andy Withers have very kindly allowed the use of pictures from their superb book *DeLorean – Celebrating the Impossible*. Thanks also go to Chris Nicholson of PJ Grady (UK) for pictures, Dan Willis who has been kind enough to allow the use of pictures of his DeLorean restoration, and John Chapelhow who has corrected all my mistakes! Other individuals who have provided photos are credited in the relevant captions, all other photos are the property of the author. And a special thanks to my long suffering wife Suzanne who puts up with my DeLorean addiction!

(Courtesy Mike Hooper)

Contents

The Essential Buyer's Guide™ currency
At the time of publication a BG unit of currency "🌑" equals approximately £1.00/US$1.35/Euro 1.13. Please adjust to suit current exchange rates using Sterling as the base currency.

1 Is it the right car for you?
– marriage guidance

The DeLorean is strictly a selfish two-seater, however it does have a generously sized boot/trunk underneath the bonnet/hood along with surprisingly ample storage behind the seats, reputably designed to accommodate a set of golf clubs!

At 13ft 8in (4.2m) long and 6ft 1in (1.86m) wide, the DeLorean will fit into a standard garage, the gullwing doors being a help in a narrow garage as the maximum amount of space required to fully open them is only 11 inches (28cm). The car is reasonably spacious, and will accommodate tall passengers with ease. It came with either a three-speed automatic or five-speed manual gearbox, the

The parcel shelf shown with removable cargo net in place. There is an often unnoticed interior light above the parcel shelf just below the rear window.

The large but shallow boot/trunk will accommodate more than you think, especially if you use 'squishy' bags. The tool kit, if supplied, would be stored in the access panel at the front of the boot/trunk.

Though the doors are often criticised they remain probably the most distinguishing feature of the car. They are far more practical than you may at first think.

The footwell of a five-speed car. Note the 'dead pedal' for your left foot, and the hood release lever (arrowed).

clutch can, however, seem heavy compared to modern standards. Power steering was never fitted, nor was it an option, so the steering can also seem a bit heavy at parking speeds. Retrofit electric power steering kits are now available. All cars came very well equipped, with air-conditioning, power mirrors and windows, a radio and tape player, central locking, leather faced seats, and a tilt/reach adjustable steering column. Driving position is very good (even as a LHD drive in the UK) and visibility is reasonable, although as a LHD it can be a little unnerving for a passenger. RHD conversion is possible but expensive. Since only small 'toll booth' windows were fitted, it is recommended that the air-conditioning works.

Left: a late 1982 grey interior, with five-speed manual gearbox, and the later style door-mounted pull straps. Centre: all of the instruments are neatly laid out, and are easy to see and read. The controls fall readily to hand. Right: only small 'toll booth' electric windows were fitted; unfortunately, they are not much use at a drive-thru!

Running costs
Buy a good car and running costs can be modest, although, as with any car, there will always be something to tinker with. Routine servicing is cheap and easy to do by the average home mechanic.

Parts availability
For a relatively low volume manufactured car, the parts availability is excellent. This is, in part, due to using a lot of 'off the shelf' parts. There are many suppliers of parts, including DMC Houston who purchased the remaining factory inventory of parts, and sells worldwide. There are also many other suppliers of new/remanufactured and replacement parts, both in the USA and Europe.

Insurance
Classic car insurers all recognise the DeLorean, and can provide very reasonably priced policies. Some give discounts if you mention being a member of an owners' club.

Investment potential
DeLoreans have for many years been seen as an ideal investment. This is one of the reasons why many suffer from long-term storage problems caused by lack of use. Values have increased substantially in the four years prior to the publication of this book. However, the author foresees values continuing to climb for some time although at a more steady rate.

The usual advice of 'buy the best you can afford' also applies to a DeLorean. The difficulty lies in buying a project car. It's difficult to budget for all of the restoration costs on a project DeLorean, which will often outweigh the price of a road-ready car. More so if you have to pay for specialists to do the work. That said, many a project car has been successfully been brought back to life by an experienced home mechanic.

Servicing
An annual check of the systems, like the UK's MoT test (brakes, chassis, suspension, steering, tyres, cooling, electrical items, etc), is a good basis and is simple to do. A basic service should be done every 3000 miles, or yearly, along with a check of all the fluid levels and vehicle condition, as well as a more major service every 15,000 miles. Coolant should be changed every two years. There are also two grease nipples on each side of the front suspension that are often overlooked. Service parts are relatively cheap, and easy to obtain from most vehicle parts suppliers and DeLorean vendors, so there is no excuse for neglect.

Spare parts
The DeLorean is very well catered for, the main inventory being available from DMC Houston. There are franchises of DMC around the US, and many independent vendors in both the US and Europe, providing original, reproduction and newly manufactured parts. Upgraded components, including suspension/chassis and braking systems, are also widely available, with great (free) advice available from these vendors. The parts listed here are just examples, and vary between suppliers/countries and over time. Prices shown are correct at time of publication, but are subject to change and taxes (the currency symbol  is explained on page 5).

A reconditioned **PRV V6** engine and five-speed gearbox about to be refitted to a club member's car, showing the exhaust cross-over pipe.

Mechanical parts

Full water hose set	●x250
Water pump	●x150 (refurbished 120)
Head gasket set	●x60
Fuel pump OE	●x75
Fuel pump – modern style including sender unit	●x400

An original fuel pump mounted in its pump support sealing ring (boot) and metal support ring. The pipe leading from the bottom of the pump goes to the in-tank mounted baffle and pickup filter. This OE pickup pipe is known for collapsing and restricting fuel flow and often has a spring inserted to prevent this.

Alternator	x160
Metering head (refurbished)	x500
Injectors (each)	x45
Clutch kit, three-piece	x170
New modern style radiator	x250
Upgraded fans	x220
Lower ball joint	x40
Angle drive	x50
Headlight	x40
Front brake pads	x17
Rear brake pads	x20
Handbrake pads	x25
Clutch slave cylinder	x35
Gas strut set (6)	x150

Body parts

RH drive conversion	x13-17,000
Passenger door torsion bar	x700
Rear wing	x1100
Front wing/fender L/H	from 1000
Rear facia (OE)	x1000
Front facia (new)	x1000
Windscreen	x400
Trailing arm bolt (TAB)	x15
S/steel engine cover grilles	x120

The Bosch K-Jet metering head and injectors. Both give long service but hate poor fuel. Those shown above have been refurbished, but this is a task best left to a specialist.

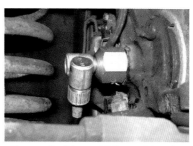

The angle drive, which provides the input to the speedometer, is located in the L/H front hub. It is often changed many times over the car's lifetime. Replacements can vary in quality and accuracy.

The clutch slave cylinder mounted at the back of the engine is difficult to see and fiddly to replace. It is worth changing this when doing the clutch master cylinder as they are best done in pairs.

Car shown with louvres raised but engine cover down, the car has stainless steel inserts rather than OE ventilation grilles. It also has an OE plastic top window finisher.

The trailing arm bolt (TAB) is often overlooked, but this safety critical component should be exchanged with an upgrade.

3 Living with a DeLorean
– will you get along together?

If you and your passenger can live with a left-hand drive car in a right-hand drive country, then the DeLorean is a great car to drive. It was never a sports car, more a 'GT' (Grand Tourer). In LHD countries, then, driving is clearly much easier. Like any car, a DeLorean is at its best when used regularly, the PRV V6 engine in DeLorean specification was de-tuned to meet US emissions regulations, so performance was not exactly blistering. Fuel economy can range from 20mpg up to 35mpg depending on transmission type and style of driving. The engine and transmission are robust, and parts are readily available to support home/DIY servicing. Daily checks are simple to do. The doors, though often criticised, are very practical, and any 'drooping' doors are usually just down to a failed gas strut that can be replaced in under a minute.

In day-to-day use the car has very good storage/luggage capabilities; a generous (but shallow) boot/trunk and the cargo net protected parcel shelf hold far more than you might think. Even the small cubby hole behind the driver's seat and the glovebox can help with storage.

When driving, all gauges are in view, and the exterior visibility is reasonable. This can, however, be improved with modern convex rear view mirrors. Driving position is good, and the car has plenty of room for tall drivers. The cabin can seem fairly dark in a black interior car, but this is down to personal

The V6 engine is easy to work on, and daily checks are all simple to perform. Access is also reasonable for any required maintenance.

The doors should stay upright without assistance, if not, check the gas strut before attempting any other adjustments. The front amber marker lights on the wings/fenders can be modified to also act as indicator side repeaters – a wise modification.

The parcel shelf can be surprisingly accommodating.

Lockable cubby box behind driver's seat is useful for secure storage or spares.

The illuminated glovebox has a nicely flocked lining but the moulded plastic insert that it is attached to can degrade and become brittle. Modern replacements are available.

1983 grey interior car's centre console. Note that no separate clock is fitted as it's incorporated into the ASI radio. Very early cars had no printing on the heater controls making them difficult to use in the daytime.

1981 grey interior car with OE digital clock fitted in 'shifter' plate.

preference. The heating and air-conditioning all work well, and road and wind noise are kept to a minimum.

The braking and suspension systems are adequate, but with many components still being original, things can be improved by simple upgrades, such as stainless steel flexible brake lines or new dampers (shock absorbers). If the car still has its original front springs fitted, then both the driving position/visibility and road handling can be improved by the fitment of new front lowering springs. It's not uncommon to see cars still on factory-fitted tyres, however this is not recommended as they will be very old and hard.

The body is easy to keep clean, yet the bane of any DeLorean owner's life is fingerprints, and they will tell you that anyone admiring a DeLorean cannot resist the urge to touch the stainless steel. There is, it seems, something about a bare metal car that must be touched. Fingerprints are, I'm afraid, part of the DeLorean experience.

The DeLorean is always an attention getter; people will walk past supercars to get to see the car and talk to the owner, simply filling with fuel can become a mini car show, and driving along, people will hang out of passing cars to take pictures (often in the DeLorean's blind spot) – just remember to smile for the camera!

The driver's view in the rear view mirror.

4 Relative values
– which model for you?

As there is basically only the one model, then values are similar. Some variations are more sought after, but this is down to personal preference rather than actual desirability. Some individuals prefer to buy an early car with a fuel filler flap, a black interior, and manual transmission. For others it may be a grey interior with automatic transmission, with a later flat hood, and others prefer any variation of the above! It really is down to personal choice. Even the wheels had minor revisions, the early wheels being dark grey in colour with a dark grey centre cap, while the later cars had silver wheels with a black centre cap. All of the centre caps feature an embossed DMC logo. The casting of the wheels also varies slightly, later wheels have a marginally deeper and thicker casting to them.

Values really come down to the type of car you're looking for; is it a non-running project, a running project car, a usable daily driver, or concours condition car? Prices vary depending on the car's actual condition rather than any other factors.

Due to the car's starring role in the *Back to the Future* films, you may also come across a DeLorean modified to look like a time machine. The value of these cars can vary enormously depending on the quality and accuracy of the work done. Because the films used a grey interior, manual transmission DeLorean, then these are sometimes the more sought after.

Left: a black interior five-speed car, note the separate digital clock fitted just in front of the gear lever, and the aftermarket stereo.

Right: an all original, late 1982 manual gearbox car with fitted black floor mats. No separate clock as it's built into the radio.

Left: the first DeLorean hoods/bonnets were produced with both a fuel filler flap and grooved 'accent' lines running down each side. Centre: the mid-style hood with the omission of the fuel filler flap, but retaining the grooved 'accent' lines down each side. Right: the final variation of hood, completely flat with an additional raised DeLorean badge on the front corner.

Non-original engines will affect the value. However, note that some have been fitted with aftermarket turbochargers, and it is down to personal preference if this is

something you require. Major changes to the interior will reduce the value, as will missing components; likewise non-original wheels will detract, as originals are expensive. In principle, the more original equipment (OE) parts that are absent, the lower the value, as some are very costly to replace.

Unique GKN cast alloy wheels were used with plastic centre caps: 14in at the front and 15in at the rear. They look great but are difficult to keep clean.

A Legend Industries prototype twin-turbo engine. Although this is very rare, several manufacturers did produce aftermarket turbos for the DeLorean, including a BAE Systems single turbo and twin IHI turbos.

5 Before you view
– be well informed

To avoid a wasted journey, and the disappointment of finding that the car does not match your expectations, it will help if you're very clear about what questions you want to ask before you pick up the telephone. Some of these points might appear basic but when you're excited about the prospect of buying your dream classic, it's amazing how some of the most obvious things slip the mind. Also check in classic car magazines for the current values of the model you are interested in, which will give both a price guide and auction results.

Where is the car?
Is it going to be worth travelling to the next county/state, or even a different country? A locally advertised car, although it may not sound very interesting, can add to your knowledge for very little effort, so make a visit – it might even be in better condition than expected. In the UK you are unlikely to find more than a few DeLoreans for sale at any one time, and many are sold through word of mouth or via 'for sale' adverts in the owners' club magazine.

Dealer or private sale
Establish early on if the car is being sold by its owner or by a trader. A private owner should have all the history, so don't be afraid to ask detailed questions. A dealer may have more limited knowledge of a car's history, but should have some documentation. A dealer may offer a warranty/guarantee (ask for a printed copy) and finance.

Cost of collection and delivery
A dealer may well be used to quoting for delivery by car transporter. A private owner may agree to meet you halfway, but only agree to this after you have seen the car at the vendor's address to validate the documents. Conversely, you could meet halfway and agree the sale, but insist on meeting at the vendor's address for the handover.

View – when and where
It is always preferable to view at the vendor's home or business premises. In the case of a private sale, the car's documentation should tally with the vendor's name and address. Arrange to view only in daylight, and avoid a wet day. Most cars look better in poor light or when wet.

Reason for sale
Do make it one of the first questions. Why is the car being sold and how long has it been with the current owner? How many previous owners?

Left-hand drive to right-hand drive
Remember, most DeLoreans were built in left-hand drive. Other than the 17 factory commissioned RHD prototypes some have since been converted to RHD cars both by skilled engineers and DeLorean specialists. If an aftermarket RHD conversion has been done it may not significantly increase the value. The DeLorean Owner's club historian should be able to confirm the history of any RHD car.

A factory-authorised RHD conversion with grey interior and automatic transmission. This car has had stainless steel letters fitted to the DMC logo on the sill.

Condition (body/chassis/interior/mechanicals)

Ask for an honest appraisal of the car's condition. An original equipment car is invariably of higher value than a customised version. Ask specifically about some of the check items described in chapter 7.

Matching data/legal ownership

Do the VIN/frame, engine numbers and licence plate match the official registration document? This would be rare with a DeLorean. Due to the location of the frame number and engine numbers this information is often omitted. If the official registration document has a section for chassis numbers, then it would often have the VIN showing rather than a frame number. What's important is for the VIN to be correct. Is the owner's name and address recorded in the official registration documents?

The frame number is affixed to the L/H side of the frame in the engine bay. The numbers may have been stamped (as shown) or hand welded.

The engine number is attached to the engine block, as indicated by the arrow. It's usually difficult to see due to the location of the catalytic converter, however in this example a de-cat pipe has been fitted.

The VIN plate, left, is attached to the driver's 'B' post. The date stamp can be embossed as shown or hand stamped (see chapter 8). The dash-mounted VIN plate, above, may either be riveted or glued in place.

For those countries that require an annual test of roadworthiness, does the car have a document showing it complies? In the UK, the appropriate MoT (Ministry of Transport) certificate can be verified online (www.gov.uk/check-mot-status) or by phone (0845 600 5977).

If the vehicle does not have a roadworthiness certificate then ensure that any import duties have been paid, and the seller has the documentation to prove this. If a smog/emissions certificate is mandatory, does the car have one?

If required, does the car carry a current road fund license/licence plate tag?

Does the vendor own the car outright? Money might be owed to a finance company or bank; the car could even be stolen. Several organisations will supply the data on ownership, based on the car's licence plate number, for a fee. Such companies can often also tell you whether the car has been 'written-off' by an insurance company. In the UK these organisations can supply vehicle data:
AA – 0344 209 0754
DVLA – 0844 306 9203
HPI – 0845 300 8905
RAC – 0800 015 6000
Other countries will have similar organisations.

Unleaded fuel
The PRV engine used in a DeLorean is designed to run on unleaded fuel. Ethanol in unleaded fuel may cause problems, however it is too early to be specific. At the current average 5% (in the UK) it may dissolve old deposits in fuel tanks and fuel lines. Ethanol may attack brass and zinc parts, the nylon fuel-injection pipe and soften flexible rubber fuel lines. The FBHVC are monitoring the situation.

Insurance
Check with your existing insurer before setting out, your current policy might not cover you to drive the car immediately if you do purchase it.

How you can pay
A cheque/check will take several days to clear and the vendor may prefer to sell to a cash buyer. However, a banker's draft (a cheque issued by a bank) is as good as cash, but safer, so contact your own bank and become familiar with the formalities that are necessary to obtain one. Please exercise caution if carrying around large sums of cash.

Buying at auction?
If the intention is to buy at auction see chapter 10 for further advice.

Professional vehicle check (mechanical examination)
There are often marque/model specialists who will undertake professional examination of a vehicle on your behalf. The DeLorean Owners' Club (UK) will be able to put you in touch with such specialists.
Other organisations that will carry out a general professional check in the UK are:
AA – 0800 056 8040 (motoring organisation with vehicle inspectors)
RAC – 0330 159 0720 (motoring organisation with vehicle inspectors)
Other countries will have similar organisations.

6 Inspection equipment

– these items will really help

This book
Reading glasses (if you need them for close work)
Torch
Probe (a small screwdriver works very well)
Overalls
Mirror on a stick
Digital camera and notebook
Trolley jack and axle stand(s)
A friend, preferably a knowledgeable enthusiast

Before you rush out of the door, gather together a few items that will help as you work your way around the car. This book is designed to be your guide at every step, so take it along and use the check boxes to help you assess each area of the car you're interested in. Don't be afraid to let the seller see you using it. Take your reading glasses if you need them to read documents and make close up inspections.

A magnet will help you check if the chassis is full of filler, however this is unlikely

and should be obvious. A torch with fresh batteries will be useful for peering into the wheelarches and under the car.

A small screwdriver can be used – with care – as a probe, to the frame particularly around the FFE (front frame extension) and engine cradle. With this, you should be able to check an area for severe corrosion, but be careful (it's not your car – yet), the screwdriver may damage the epoxy coating on the chassis and may go right through to the metal!

The screwdriver is also a useful tool to check the roof box section that you can see, but do NOT damage or mark the torsion bar in any way. Be prepared to get dirty. Take along a pair of overalls, if you have them. Fixing a mirror at an angle on the end of a stick may seem odd, but you'll probably need it to check the condition of the underside of the car. It will also help you to peer into some of the important crevices. You can also use it, together with the torch, along the underside of the car and on the floor.

If you have the use of a digital camera, take it along so that later you can study some areas of the car more closely. Take a picture of any part of the car that causes you concern, and seek a friend's or owner's opinion.

Ideally, have a friend or knowledgeable enthusiast accompany you: a second opinion is always valuable. The DeLorean Owners' Club is always happy to help out with advising on any potential purchase.

A restored rolling chassis, very much as OE with the exception of a modern radiator and stainless steel sheaved flexible brake lines. Below: the same rolling chassis but from the rear, again virtually as stock, however modern shock absorbers/dampers have been fitted.

7 Fifteen minute evaluation
– walk away or stay?

It's hard not to be taken in by a DeLorean on first viewing, it may be that this is the first time you have seen a DeLorean up close. However, you need to exercise sound judgement, and look with your head rather than your heart. It helps if the seller thinks that you are a serious potential purchaser rather than a 'tyre kicker,' or someone who just wishes to see, sit-in, or have a ride in a DeLorean. Good communication and asking the right questions prior to viewing will always help you to be taken seriously. Please also remember that this is not your car, would you like someone prodding and poking at your car with a screwdriver? Exercise care and caution. It's worthwhile asking why the seller is selling the vehicle; is it a genuine reason, does the seller actually own the car they are trying to sell? Do the vehicle documents match the VIN? Ideally, use this section in conjunction with chapter 9 as most points are covered as you take a tour around the car.

Start with the backbone of the car, the chassis. If possible try to arrange to have the vehicle raised slightly to help with inspection, but don't be tempted to go underneath a car that's not properly supported on stands. The chassis/frame is difficult to see, particularly if the front has been lowered. The main rot sections are around the front frame extension (FFE) and on the engine cradle at the rear of the frame (see page 26). All DeLoreans should have been fitted with a 'recall kit' that is attached to the FFE and anti-roll bar/sway bar (indicated by the black brackets arrowed). It is vital that these be fitted if not already present, but the parts are readily available. Look out for leaks around the brake or clutch master cylinder and reservoir, the fluid can dissolve the epoxy coating, allowing the frame or fuel tank closing plate to rust. Minor scrapes on the epoxy are not unusual, and this is easy to touch-up with the appropriate paint. A lot of the late 1982-83 cars had an underseal sprayed onto the frame for extra protection, and, more often than not, covering everything else surrounding it!

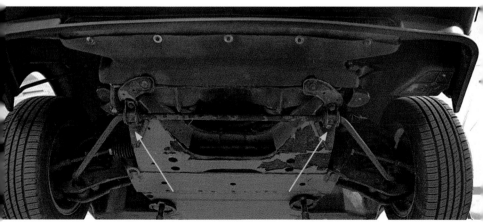

Corrosion can be extensive on the FFE. Check that the front end recall kit has been fitted as shown by the black brackets (arrowed). (Courtesy Alex Manos, Beverly Hills Car Club)

Now, the matter of the stainless steel … The panel gaps were never perfect from the factory, so their condition is more important. Panels can discolour and become dull, but can be restored easily. Look for dents and damage, as these can be expensive and time-consuming to repair. Do the doors open and close smoothly? To close, it's best to press in the centre of the door just beneath the window. Don't worry if the doors 'droop' slightly when open it's probably just down to a failed gas strut – these work differently depending on ambient temperature and are simple to replace, they should be considered a consumable item. Whilst checking the door area, look along and behind the torsion bar area for signs of corrosion of the roof box. Do NOT be tempted to prod, poke or scratch the torsion bar, as these are very easily damaged. Also look along the back of the roof 'T' panel along the top of the louvres, does this look straight? Ask to have the rear louvres opened, and look along the roof line below the 'T' panel and above the rear screen as the roof box can separate in this area. This is difficult to see as it's behind the upper screen finisher. Whilst not a difficult repair, it may be a bargaining point; of far more importance is corrosion in the roof box area (see chapter 9).

The original plastic upper screen finisher itself may be missing or damaged, or may have had a stainless steel replacement fitted.

The door hinge and torsion bar area (shown with the door seal removed). Check very carefully along and below the torsion bar for any signs of corrosion. This cryogenically frozen and twisted bar gives most of the required force to lift the door, the gas struts simply support the door when raised.

Extensive corrosion of the lower roof box area. The roof box inspection/electrical plug access hole is visible top right. This area is usually covered by the stainless steel 'T' panel.

Are the rear louvres and engine cover intact and undamaged? The louvres can break between the ribs along the centre spine (reinforcing kits are available), and the engine cover can become damaged by attempts to close it with the engine cover stay still in place.

Are the facias intact and undamaged? Missing and/or damaged exterior trim can be expensive to replace. Looking at the engine from above, do all the normal checks (on a cold engine) as you would to any car, check the coolant for any oil mixing, likewise the oil filler cap for signs of 'mayonnaise' that may indicate a blown head gasket(s). Check the oil for level and condition. Looking around the lower (L/H) side of the engine check for a leak from the oil pressure

The upper screen finisher shown in place. It's easier to see any roof box separation with this removed. The originals were black plastic, unlike the stainless steel one that's fitted here. This car also features an aftermarket high level brake light.

With the upper screen finisher removed you can see its mounting bracket (arrowed on the left) and the end of torsion bar (arrowed on the right). It's along the base of this metal box section that you may see 'roof box separation.' The upper screen finisher should be installed as it holds down the roof 'T' panel.

A typical cracked louvre with the stainless steel reinforcing brace on the side.

Newly fitted water pump. The arrow shows the drain hole.

sensor – this is a common failure, but a cheap and easy fix. Look for leaks close to the base of the water pump. There may be an occasional drip from the water pump drain, any signs of a large oil leak coming from below the water pump could indicate serious issues. This is a good time to check the frame and engine number (if you can see it behind the catalytic converter). There is a large 'O' ring close to the air conditioning compressor, attached to the timing cover, that can leak oil: again this should not be confused with a major block oil leak. To the R/H side of the engine are the starter/oil filter/ oil pressure sender (gauge) and the alternator. A newly fitted oil filter would be a good indicator of a recent service.

Have the vendor start the car and continue your checks. The odd-fire PRV engine in a DeLorean can have a fairly lumpy idle, so don't worry about this, particularly if the engine is cold. Are there any water leaks/odd noises? Look around the engine again to check for anything obviously wrong or leaking. As the engine warms up, look along the underside of the car for leaks from the cooling system and radiator. Check the temperature gauge, the cooling fans should operate when the temperature gauge on the dashboard reaches between one third and halfway (if the gauge goes beyond the halfway mark, then it would be wise to turn the engine off). When happy, turn the engine off and turn your attention to the interior, with the engine switched off it's common for the gauges to indicate that it is still running, the tachometer will often show 1000rpm regardless. The odometer trip button is often missing or broken, but can be easily replaced; gauges can be erratic or appear faulty, but this issue is usually just down to a damaged or decaying circuit board (or possibly a bad earth) – again modern replacements are available, and it's an easy fix.

Does the speedo work? The angle drive (page 9), dust shields, cables and lambda counter box for the speedometer are common failure points. As it's not unusual for any part of this system to have failed over the years, use the indicated mileage only as a guide. The lambda counter was designed to illuminate a light on the dashboard at the recommended interval to change the oxygen sensor in the OE exhaust system, and should be reset at every 30,000 miles. The components used in the speedometer system are relatively cheap, but their overall reliability can be improved by removing the lambda counter.

Interior
Missing parts are more of a problem than either worn or damaged elements. The sun can play havoc with the interior of a car, instrument binnacles and dashboards may have become brittle and cracked, the OE dashboards had punched speaker holes at either end. Either the binnacle or the dashboard may have been re-trimmed to various standards, but new dashboards are now available.

The R/H side of engine showing the alternator (top left) then from L-R, oil pressure sender (gauge), oil filter and starter motor. Above the starter motor is the R/H exhaust manifold and 'stove plate' to direct hot air to air filter intake. The earthing cable which is just below the starter and attached to the frame can break or lose continuity causing electrical issues.

The lambda counter box in the driver's footwell. It is not required for UK regulations, so it can be removed and bypassed with a one-piece speedometer cable, thereby eliminating one of the many components.

Early five-speed grey interior car showing extensive sun damage to the dashboard and the instrument binnacle (Courtesy Alex Manos, Beverly Hills Car Club).

A steering wheel without the usual leather wrapping.

A later car, without the lockable fuel filler, shown with all of the caps removed. On the left is simply a drain hole, centre is the fuel filler, and on the right is the clutch fluid reservoir (if fitted).

The brake fluid reservoir, below the boot carpet, shown with the dust cap removed. Originals had a float mechanism built into the cap, with electrical connections for low fluid level warning.

Trim pieces may have become damaged over the years, but most are repairable or replaceable. Check in the passenger footwell for dampness, this could indicate a leaking heater matrix, or simply a blocked drain from the heater box.

The seat covers may be beyond repair, but new ones are available. The steering wheels were (with a few exceptions) leather wrapped, the underneath had a textured finish so it's not always immediately noticeable if it's missing. Grab the steering wheel, does the steering column move at all? This is usually down to a failed bushing where the column goes through the body tub, however it may also be a broken collapsible cage on the column. The steering wheel is both a tilt and telescopic adjustable unit, operated via a plastic knob on the R/H side of the column, the thread of which can become stripped and not tighten up fully.

Open the hood/trunk and check the levels and cleanliness of both the brake and clutch fluid (if equipped); are all of the rubber bungs/dust caps fitted? The vehicle's tool kit should be in the compartment accessed at the front of the trunk area, and is a bonus if it's still with the car. It's not unusual (and is recommended) that a secondary backup cable for the hood release be fitted, as originals often fail, this is best routed to the inside of the vehicle for security.

Try to check the body tub, as you move around the car, for signs of previous repairs. This is often difficult to see, however, due to the fact that most of it is covered up either by the facias or stainless steel panels. At each side of the engine bay, and behind the rear wing glass, is an area called the pontoon: early cars have a textured finish here, whereas later cars have a smooth finish.

If not a project car, is the car driveable? If so, ask the vendor to take you on a test drive. How well does the car accelerate, change gear, handle and stop? An honest vendor should have no issues with a demonstration if they think you are a serious buyer. Ask to include a mix of roads both in town and on faster stretches, so you can see how the car moves through the gears, and how it behaves in slower traffic. Upon your return, insist on leaving the car idling for at least 10 minutes. This will give you time to have another look around and underneath the car for leaks, and to ensure that the cooling fans are operating correctly and the vehicle is not overheating. Again, this is a good time to check that the cooling fans operate before the temperature gauge reaches the halfway point, and that the coolant temperature goes down when the fans are operating.

Front hood release mechanism, note that a secondary backup cable has been fitted.

An early body tub with 'textured' pontoon. (Courtesy John Chapelhow)

The smooth body tub on top of the rear pontoon.

8 Key points

– where to look for problems

The first priority is to establish exactly what's being offered. There are good online records covering the relatively small number of cars produced. Using these, a simple VIN check can establish if the car was originally produced as a manual/automatic and black/grey interior. The frames for a manual and automatic are different, and considerable resource is required to change a vehicle from one to the other, both in time and parts. DeLoreans often change hands fairly quickly for various reasons, particularly if the car is a recent import of a dealer.

Items to check

Ownership history: few owners is good, and long-term ownership (with regular use) is better. Full history and photos/documentation/invoices of work done are a real bonus. If the vendor has had work done to the car, or had new parts fitted, then they should have these receipts at the very least. Early history, particularly on an imported car, can be sketchy.

Check that the vehicle's documentation matches the VIN plates; both on the driver's door edge and the dashboard. The dashboard VIN may be

The VIN plate fitted to the 'B' post of an early car, see also the later variation on page 15. (Courtesy John Chapelhow)

The PRV engine with a stock exhaust system showing its cast iron manifold (top) and OE catalytic converter. The engine number location is arrowed, and, inset, a close up of the number, affixed to the block.

riveted or glued in place. The frame number is on a plate attached to the rear of the chassis, the numbers may be stamped or handwritten, welded onto a separate plate that's then welded to the frame (page 15).

The frame number is never the same as the VIN, and was not recorded by the factory – they are often close, but not identical. Likewise, due to the relatively inaccessible position of the engine number, it's often not recorded on vehicle documentation.

The frame, this is the backbone of the car, it would be normal to ask for pictures of this area before viewing. Satisfy yourself that the frame is in a reasonable condition, or the condition you are expecting, before going any further. The roof box area is a mild steel boxed section, that runs from the windscreen to the rear window. This can separate along the rear edge, or, in the worst-case scenario, heavily corrode. It's a difficult area to inspect without removing the stainless 'T' panel, but having someone open the doors while you watch for movement at the rear of the roof is a good start. See chapter 9 for more information.

The stainless steel: is it without dents/creases/tears? Some damage can be expensive to have professionally repaired.

Engine: does the engine run smoothly without strange knocking noises or leaking fluids? If it's a project car **DON'T** be tempted to simply try to put new fuel in, and spin it over to see if it will start, nor even put a battery on the car, until all of the fuel system has been cleaned out. See chapter 15, K-Jet system.

Rear engine cradle lower sections, corrosion can be extensive to the box sections in this area if it has been allowed to take hold, trailing arm shields shown in place. (Courtesy Alex Manos, Beverly Hills Car Club)

9 Serious evaluation
– 60 minutes for years of enjoyment

You will be buying a DeLorean because you want one, not because it exactly fits your transport needs. That said, it is a far more practical car than you may at first think. Though it may be difficult, due to your location, or the amount of actual DeLoreans in the country you live in, it's best practice to view as many DeLoreans as you can prior to committing a large amount of money.

A second set of eyes is always useful, as they can point out any items that you might miss, and to remind you to inspect certain points and key areas that you may not notice, especially if this is the first DeLorean you are viewing.

Remember also that the owners' club will always help with pre-purchase advice, and may be able to put you in touch with a local owner to assist in an inspection. DeLorean specialists can also perform a professional inspection for a fee, which may be beneficial, particularly if you are purchasing a vehicle in another country. The best way to use this section is to tick the boxes as you go along, as it may be difficult to remember all of the details of the vehicle when you sit down to think about it later on.

The following sections are specifically tailored to the DeLorean – their particular weaknesses, and highlighting the variations that occurred during the production run. Score each section as follows: Excellent (4), Good (3), Average (2), or Poor (1), being as realistic as possible.

General appearance and fit
[4] [3] [2] [1]

Look carefully at the car from each side, then from the front and rear. Does it 'sit' well? How are the panel gaps? DeLoreans often had poor panel gaps when new, especially on 'early' cars. As most panels are easily detached, time and patience can improve the fit and finish. Early cars had a two key system; the door key also fitting the fuel cap and a separate ignition key.

Locks
[4] [3] [2] [1]

Later cars had just a single key system and no locking fuel cap. Usually an early car with two keys would have a gas flap hood with locking fuel filler cap, but often hoods are swapped around due to owner preference, or possibly accident damage. It is possible for a specialist to fit a fuel flap to a hood if this is something that you specifically require.

The lockable fuel filler cap on an early car fitted with fuel filler flap on the hood.

Chassis/frame
[4] [3] [2] [1]

Start with the backbone of the car, the chassis. If possible try to arrange to have the vehicle raised, or hire a vehicle lift at a self-service repair centre or garage to help with inspection. The chassis is difficult to see, particularly if the front has been lowered, the frame originally covered in a two-part epoxy to provide corrosion protection has stood the test of time well, however this can crack and admit water,

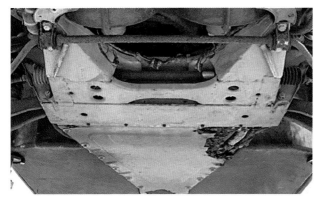

causing rot. The main rot sections are around the front frame extension (FFE) and on the engine cradle at the rear of the frame (see chapter 8, page 26). If the brake or clutch master cylinder have leaked this can dissolve the epoxy on the frame, allowing rust to take hold on the frame or on the fuel tank cover plate. It's not unusual to have minor scrapes on the epoxy, especially in the section in between the front wheels, as this is the section that can be 'caught' by speed humps and the like. Providing the metal is undamaged then it's easy to touch up with appropriate paint. Moving along the frame again, check the area below the clutch and brake master cylinders (behind the left front wheel).

Trailing arms

4 3 2 1

Moving along to the rear of the chassis check the condition of the trailing arms, these are also made from mild steel, and covered in epoxy like the frame. Ask when (or if) there is any record of the trailing arm bolts (TABs) having been changed. These bolts are often neglected, and should have been changed for modern replacements (available from vendors). These are often found to be bent and corroded, and have been known to fail on rare occasions. Below this area should be large trailing arm shields on either side of the chassis, between the main chassis rail and body tub. These are sometimes missing after having been removed for repair work, or due to the retaining studs on the bodytub having been

The trailing arm bolt (TAB) location, flexible brake line from the frame to the trailing arm is also shown.

broken or sheared off. This, however, is a simple repair with new metal strips with welded on studs simply being fitted from within the cubby box and battery box floor location.

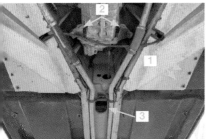

Trailing arm shields showing the fixing nuts (1). The gearbox (five-speed) mounting brackets (2), and access hole in the frame (3) where the 'bell crank' assembly and fuel accumulator are fitted.

Wheels

Wheels can be refurbished by alloy wheel specialists, but replacements are expensive, so treat them carefully. It's advised that the wheels are removed and fitted without the use of impact wrenches, as these have been known to damage the wheels, wheel studs and wheel nuts. The wheel nut torque is just 60lb-ft/80Nm. It's also worthwhile checking the date codes on the tyres. How old are they? Often DeLoreans are found to be still running around on the original factory fitted tyres. Whilst looking at the front wheels, try to find out what, if any, work has been done to the front suspension.

Front suspension

The lower control arms (LCAs) were manufactured from thin gauge steel, and in many cases are found to have some minor damage from either incorrect jacking or towing. The arms may have had plates welded along the bottom, or may have been replaced with a solid aluminium item. Ideally, the ball joints in the LCAs should have been changed to modern UK made ones. There have been instances of original ball joints failing; since substitutes can vary in quality if the history is unknown then it's a wise precaution to change them.

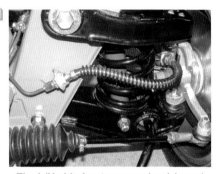

The L/H side front suspension (viewed from the front) in completely original configuration.

Both original and replacement top and bottom ball joints have a grease nipple fitted, and have often been neglected. The original shock absorbers (front and rear) are easily identifiable by being light grey in colour and having the word

UK-manufactured lower ball joints.

'Girling' embossed on them. These have lasted very well, but have often been replaced by the likes of Spax/Pro-Tech/AVO/DMC and many others. Some perform better than others, and a lot is down to personal preference.

Rear suspension

The rear suspension is very robust, many cars are still running around on the original springs and shock absorbers, and performing perfectly adequately on them. Modern replacements are available depending on your preference and budget.

The L/H side rear suspension (viewed from the rear).

Stainless steel

The body panels are made from grade 304 stainless steel, the panels can discolour and become dull, but can be restored easily. You're looking for dents and damage. The odd small dent does occur to the body, however lots of dents/damage/creases to the bodywork can be expensive and time-consuming to repair. Contrary to popular belief, stainless steel can corrode, resulting in a 'pitted' surface.

Doors

Do the doors open and close smoothly? The door lock 'cut outs' and guides varied slightly through production. Early doors have a small 'U' shaped cut out with metal door guides, later doors have a more triangular shape with plastic door guides. To close, from the outside, it's best to press in the centre of the door just below the window glass. While in this area, check to see if the lower door strut mounting bracket attached to the body tub is bent. This bracket, which holds the gas strut to the bodytub, is fairly weak and can 'pull' out of the body tub. There are several reinforcing brackets available, and the one pictured on the right is one of the best.

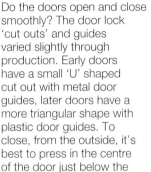

Left: an early door with the 'U' shaped door lock cut-outs and metal door guides. The doors are fitted with three marker lights; amber lights facing forward and on the base of the door, and a red light to the rear. Right: a later door with the 'V' shaped door lock cut-outs and plastic door guides. The marker lights are commonly refitted with LEDs to minimise battery drain.

Left: heavily corroded bent and broken door strut mounting bracket. Note the originals were only fixed to the body tub in two locations. Right: new door strut mounting bracket. This spreads the load over a greater surface area of the GRP and is a massive improvement.

Roof box

When checking the door area, look all the way along and behind the torsion bar area for any signs of corrosion of the roof box. Do NOT be tempted to prod, poke or scratch the torsion bar as these are very easily damaged. Whilst in this area, look along the back of the roof 'T' panel along the top of the louvres, does this look

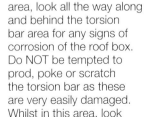

Left: heavy corrosion to the rear of the roof box, note the inspection hole at the top. The cover was missing allowing water to enter. Right: the roof box with corroded sections removed. The wiring for all of the door electrical connections can be seen.

straight? The roof box can separate along the rear edge, and although not a difficult repair, as it simply involves bolting the area back down, it may be a bargaining point. Of far more importance is corrosion in the roof box area. This is expensive to repair and usually involves removing the doors and 'T' panel, then removing the corroded roof box and replacing with a new stainless steel one. This is perhaps best left to a specialist, but can be done by home mechanics. The roof box is difficult to assess fully with the 'T' panel fitted to the car. Ideally, this should be removed for a full inspection, but clearly this may not be practical, and would no doubt be

A rear roof box section repair. If it's in good condition then it only requires the two sections bolting back together. A good time to inspect the rest of the roof box area and apply corrosion protection to the inside.

frowned upon by the vendor! The more time spent examining this area the better.

Engine cover/rear louvres

Are the rear louvres, the engine cover and the mesh grilles within the engine cover all intact and undamaged? These can all be expensive to replace, but a choice of stainless steel or OE mesh grilles are available. The engine cover is sometimes damaged due to attempts to close before the engine cover 'stay' has been properly unhooked.

Car shown with louvres raised but engine cover down, this car has the original ventilation mesh grilles.

Front and rear facias

Subtle changes occurred in both colour and finish (glossy/matt) throughout the production run. The facias are made of a urethane material, and have stood the test of time well. The main issue is with the front facia, which can develop 'eyebrows' – a warping over the inner headlights. This can be rectified by removing the facia, heating the area and placing a thin flat bar under the top of the facia and bonding it all together whilst keeping the area flat. Check also that the lower spoiler and 'rock screen' in front of the radiator are intact and undamaged. Painting the facias is a more specialist task, as getting paint adhesion can be an issue. The original DeLorean logo on the rear facia was originally left bare, but has often had in-fill letters fitted, and sometimes painted. The rear lights are unique to the car,

Warping above the inner headlights ('eyebrows') is common on the front facia, is an easy if time consuming fix. The headlights themselves are poor compared to a modern vehicle, and upgrades are limited (in the UK) due to the size of the headlights and lighting regulations.

and are often found with faded indicator sections, these can be painted or replaced. Originally fitted with four brake lights, the inner brake lights are often converted (for UK use) to fog lights whilst retaining the brake light facility. The rear light circuit boards can also fail, but these can either be refurbished or new replacements are available. The number plate surrounds were manufactured using an ERM (elastic reservoir moulding) process, and designed to be used with US-style number plates. These have sometimes been changed to accommodate a Euro-style number plate, but is not compulsory for UK use.

Engine

Looking at the engine again, the oil pressure sensor will probably be leaking oil, but it's a cheap and easy fix. Check for leaks around the base of the water pump. Signs of a large oil leak coming from below the water pump and above the crank pulley could indicate serious block rot. This is a problem that has become apparent in the last few years, where the aluminium will corrode in the centre of the 'V' of the engine, often at the bottom of the casting holes. The area is well hidden beneath the intake manifold, and has become known in DeLorean circles as the 'valley of death' (VOD). There are also several water pipes running along this area that can leak, this combined with dirt/debris can accelerate corrosion to the engine block. Damage can sometimes be repaired by having plates welded over the areas affected, however it's not always successful. Prevention is better than cure, and can be achieved by ensuring that the area is regularly cleaned out and any leaks dealt with. Some people use an engine paint to protect the area from further corrosion.

There is an 'O' ring behind the camshaft pulley plate, close to the A/C compressor pulley, that can lose a small amount of oil. Again, this is an easy fix, so don't confuse this with a larger oil leak from within the engine

A large amount of oil leaking from this area, above the crank pulley and just below the water pump, could be evidence of 'block rot.'

The amber colouring in the rear indicators can fade with age. Many owners have fitted stainless steel insert letters to highlight 'DeLorean' on the rear facia.

Oil leaks can often be found from and around this oil pressure sensor, a common problem but a cheap and easy fix. Note that this engine is fitted with a high performance exhaust system, this really tidies up the engine bay.

The bottom of the engine valley: corrosion can occur in any of the casting holes along this area. Some of these casting holes are up to 8.5cm deep into the engine block.

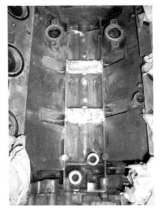

An engine block with the deeper holes welded over. This engine had block rot through to an oil gallery, but was fixed with this repair.

valley. There are two 'idler pulleys' in this area that guide the A/C drivebelt. The bearings in these fail due to heat from the exhaust below. These can make a lot of noise when failing, and it's not always easy to identify where the noise is coming from, but, again, these are a very simple and cheap fix. Look around the engine again to check for anything obviously wrong or leaking.

The 'O' ring behind this camshaft cover plate can leak; don't confuse this with an oil leak from the valley of the engine.

Engine bay ④ ③ ② ①

The original air intake system was a bit convoluted, consisting of a valve to direct warm air from above the R/H exhaust manifold when the engine was cold, or from outside the car in warmer weather. This is often exchanged with a simple air intake pipe to tidy up the area, and allow for a less restricted airflow. Check for blowing exhaust manifold gaskets, this being a common failure. The rest of the exhaust system, whilst somewhat restrictive, works well with a combination of cast iron manifolds/cross over pipe/single

An OE air filter intake system. The large metal pipe goes down to a stove plate fitted over the R/H side exhaust manifold.

catalytic converter, and a grade 409 stainless steel silencer (muffler). The engine may have had its OE exhaust system replaced with a 'performance' exhaust: these vary in style from different manufacturers in both the US and UK.

The header/overflow bottle: the originals were a moulded plastic unit; over time

Left: a 'performance' air intake pipe fitted, this goes through the R/H pontoon to the rear induction grille. Note stainless steel header bottle tank. Right: variation of a 'performance' air intake pipe. This vehicle is fitted with an OE header tank and is starting to degrade on the R/H side.

these have become brittle and have been known to fail. Many have been replaced with various styles, often in stainless steel, though modern plastic ones are also available. Two types of alternator were fitted, the first was an 80amp Ducellier, and then, when this was found to be insufficient, a 90amp Motorola was fitted. Many original units are still in use and working fine, however if a replacement is required OE units are hard to find, so many have now been changed.

Fuel and ignition

The original fuel-injection lines were made of black thermoplastic, covered with a protective rubber outer. These have been known to fail, and are often replaced with modern plastic or stainless steel ones. The fuel distributor/metering head is not regarded as a user serviceable item, and should be left to a specialist company. To the left, and fed by the fuel distributor, is a cold start valve – essentially another fuel injector that acts as an enrichment device when the engine is cold. The ignition distributor is behind

OE fuel injection lines, with the engine cover support/stay (arrowed).

and below the fuel distributor, it is difficult to see/access, and is therefore often overlooked during routine servicing. The car runs best on the original Bosch HR6DS sparkplugs.

Bottom left: the R/H side rear of the engine bay with the coil cover in place. Left: the same area with the cover removed, showing the coil location (OE coil) and the electrical multiplugs. Corrosion can occur on the 'pins' within the multiplugs causing electrical issues.

To the rear R/H side of the engine bay is the ignition coil and a group of electrical connections. There should be a cover over it, but this didn't fit well, and may have become brittle over time, so is often missing.

Cooling

The otterstat (switches the cooling fans on and off) and the coolant pipe that it's mounted in, is to the left hand side of the engine, and is usually attached to the frame. This can be a weak point in the cooling system, and can fail without warning. It's a cheap and simple part to replace, but recently a more reliable, full replacement pipe with screw-in otterstat became an option. Check the dashboard temperature gauge prior to having the engine started. While the engine warms up, look along the underside of the car for leaks from the cooling system and radiator. Often, there will be seepage from the side tanks of the radiator if the original is still fitted. Also check that all shrouds and ducting is in place and undamaged. Watch the temperature gauge to ensure it rises as the engine warms; the cooling fans should kick in before the halfway point. Check that both fans operate. The original fans are pictured below, however many owners have fitted new modern replacements, often at the same time as fitting a replacement radiator. These help reduce the load on the electrical system, and increase cooling efficiency.

An OE 'push-in' otterstat (fan switch) in an OE coolant pipe, and spare otterstat switch in front. Below: a newer style fan switch and pipe, with an improved screw-in otterstat.

Left: it's really important that all of the cooling shrouds are in place and undamaged, as shown here, from the front of the radiator to the air intake below the bumper (modern style radiator fitted).

OE fans removed from the car: the surround can start to break up and crumble with age.

Left: modern 'pancake' fans fitted in a custom-made housing designed to fit both OE and new radiators.

Interior

What's the condition of the interior? Missing parts are more of an issue than either sun-damage or general wear and tear. Carpets varied in colour, initially aligning to the interior colour, dark grey for black interior cars, and light grey for grey interiors, eventually both black and grey cars had light grey carpets, all had a moulded rubber foot mat under the driver's pedals. The carpets have stood the test of time and usually clean up well, but new replacement sets are available if required.

Battery/battery box

Whilst in the cabin check the battery (behind the passenger seat) for condition and signs of leaking, many cars have suffered leaking batteries in the past, resulting in damage to the carpets and battery securing strap. The original battery used screw-in side terminals, which will often have been changed to top-mounted terminal versions. A battery isolator is a common addition for security and to prevent parasitic drains.

The battery box behind the passenger seat, shown here with the cover placed above for illustration. This car has a battery isolator switch, which is a common modification. It is rare to have the battery retaining strap still in place.

Parcel shelf

The parcel shelf should have a cargo net fitted, but it is often missing. The release for the engine cover is to the L/H side just below the window, along with a speaker behind the trim panel. The parcel shelf carpet should match the colour of the rest of the carpet, and can be carefully peeled back

The engine cover release lever (arrowed), in a grey interior car. The rear speaker location is also shown.

to reveal two removable plywood panels covering all the vehicle's electrical systems.

Interior electrics

To the L/H side of the parcel shelf is the ignition ECU/lamda ECU and idle speed ECU, all are reliable. You will often find a relay for the electric aerial if the rear-mounted one is fitted.

To the R/H side, and above the battery, is the fuse box and relay compartment. After 35 years, time and previous owners can wreak havoc with the electrical systems. Fuses (usually for the fuel pump) and the surrounding holder can melt. New fuse boxes are available, as are relay/fuse kits. A missing relay in the furthest left relay holder that has been replaced with a simple three branch wire is a factory modification.

Ignition/lamda and idle speed ECU's, along with a relay for a fog light and wiring for rear mounted aerial. There may also be additional relays/alarm modules depending on owner modifications.

The larger black box is the door lock module, and the relays in this box can fail, resulting in a drain to the battery. Updated control modules and door lock solenoids are available to cure this. On the tray underneath the door lock module are two more relays along with the fuel pump relay.

Whilst inside the car, check that both window motors work (down and up) and that the switches/blower motor/lights/wipers/washers/clock (if a separate item) all work. Do

An OE fuse box in good condition would have originally had a cover, but is best left off to help prevent heat build-up.

the original radio and, if fitted, electric aerial both work? The shifter panel-mounted OE clocks on early cars have often failed, but they are rare and may have been changed to a modern equivalent. The control wheel on the shifter panel in front of the gear stick is a rheostat that controls the dashboard lights. However, if the dashboard lights have been replaced with LEDs, then this will no longer work correctly.

Three versions of radio were fitted during the production run. The first two were manufactured by a company called Craig, the last by a company called ASI. The Craig radios had a digital display on the tape door (often broken), the early ones displayed the radio frequency only, the later ones also showed the time, allowing the deletion of a separate clock. The ASI has a DMC logo on the tape door, and a built-in clock. Many cars have had aftermarket radios fitted, as both the original radios and speakers are often regarded as poor compared to modern sound systems. Original radios are both expensive and difficult to obtain.

The driver's door showing power mirror adjuster and central locking rocker switch.

Moving to the driver's seat, close the door. This is best done using the door grab handle, the pull straps are only there to assist in closing the door to the point where the handle can be reached. The leather pull straps were not initially fitted to the doors. The practical need meant this was soon corrected; early cars used a simple leather pull strap with a metal loop fitted around the grab handle. Later cars used an integrated pull strap incorporated into the door trim.

Check to see if the central locking works on both doors, using the switch in the door; only do this with both doors shut. Also, check the power mirrors both work in all directions. The plastic trim piece around this area (called an escutcheon) is often found to be damaged and broken, but new ones are available.

Instrumentation

Check to see if all the gauges work (page 7) as they should. Original speedometers showed a maximum speed of 85mph, a US requirement at the time, with a highlighted 55mph; all the gauges read in imperial measurements. Cars originally supplied to Canada and the UAE had metric clusters with the speedometers marked in KM/H and with metric measurements on all of the gauges. The UK specification RHD cars had a rare (and somewhat optimistic) 140mph speedometer. OE speedometers can be altered to show a variety of measurements (usually to 160mph). The speedometer you may have famously seen show 88mph on the *BTTF* time machine was especially mocked up for the film.

Headlinings [4] [3] [2] [1]

Look above you at the headlining, originally it would have been dark or light grey fitted to black and grey cars respectively. Late 1982-1983 cars were all fitted with light grey headlinings, these are in four pieces – one attached to each door and two sections attached to the roof. The headlinings will likely have been re-covered, as the original foam-backed material that was glued to the fibreboard headliners disintegrates over time, resulting in sagging. Similarly, water leaks from the many door seals in this area doesn't help the headlinings. If the fibreboards are in good condition then they can all be retrimmed and reinstalled. Modern fibreglass backing boards are available, should yours be beyond refurbishment. Sun visors can also suffer the same fate, and are interchangeable from side to side. New replacements in light and dark grey are available.

The headliners, consist of four pieces; one on each door and two attached to the roof.

Comfort & convenience [4] [3] [2] [1]

After the engine has been off for about 10 minutes, check to see if it restarts normally. This is a good way to check if the car has a 'hot start' problem, usually caused by a failing fuel accumulator. Does the air-conditioning work? If you don't know how to do it, ask the seller to switch on the air-conditioning, and check to see if the A/C compressor clutch is cutting in and out, and if it blows cold air from the vents.

Boot/trunk [4] [3] [2] [1]

Open the hood. On early cars there is a hole cut on the direct opposite side to the washer bottle filler with a blanking cap, this is omitted on later cars. The washer bottle is housed within a separate GRP section that is fitted to the body tub. This moulding

An air conditioning compressor. The very end plate of the compressor (arrowed) will rotate if the A/C is working. Expect to see it cycle on and off, if it does not it may indicate a fault in the A/C system or simply that it's low on gas.

has inadequate drain holes that can become blocked, resulting in a failed washer pump motor. If not already done then larger drain holes should be drilled in this.

Lift the trunk carpet, there may or may not be a separate piece of hardboard covering the spare wheel area. Is the spare supplied? It should be a cast aluminium space saver. Note that, even if you ever choose to use a 35-year-old spare, the rear 15in road wheel doesn't actually fit in the void!

An early body tub showing the extra hole in the tub (top right), with a rubber blanking cap. A washer bottle fitted with a metal cap is also common on early cars. (Courtesy John Chapelhow)

The space saver spare, useful but, being at least 35 years old would you want to use it?

Windscreen

The air intake for the ventilation system is just below the windscreen in front of the passenger seat, and directly above the heater matrix. This is why it's important that the drain does not become blocked. Whilst looking in this area, have a look at the windscreen. Is it in good condition and not delaminating? These are readily available, so it's not a major issue if cracked. On early cars the aerial for the radio was built in to the windscreen. It was moved to improve reception, initially to the front R/H wing, and then to the location where it is on most, in the rear L/H induction grille. The R/H induction grille is the air intake for the engine that feeds the air filter. On the factory RHD cars the aerial was mounted on the roof at the front of the 'T' panel. The black paint on the windscreen surrounds can peel, but these can be easily removed and re-painted.

The air intake for the heating and air conditioning just below the windscreen on the R/H side.

An early car with the windscreen mounted aerial.

The rear mounted, electrically retractable aerial within the rear L/H pontoon, it extends out of the rear induction grille.

Test drive

Will the vendor allow you to drive the car, and are you fully insured to do so? It may be better to be the passenger, so that you can pay close attention to how the car sounds and feels, rather than have to concentrate on driving an unfamiliar vehicle. Is the car safe and legal to drive? If so, the vendor should be willing to give you a test drive.

Gearbox

If it's an automatic, does the gearbox shift up and down smoothly without having to use the shifter? Does it hold in any gear for longer than it should? If so, it may be that it simply needs an oil flush and filter change, or that the gear change computer/governor inside has failed – a not uncommon problem, and easily fixed, but left neglected will damage the transmission. If it's a five-speed manual, do the gears engage smoothly without any undue grating or noise? Does the car move between gears smoothly? If not, it may be that the linkage is simply in need of adjustment, or the pivot bolt in the centre of the frame has become worn

A pivot bolt and bell crank; the pivot bolt can wear resulting in 'vague' gear changes. At worst it can snap, resulting in no gears.

and needs replacing. Is there any 'whining,' particularly on over-run? And don't forget to check for a reverse gear! Also listen for unusual noises from the drive shafts and constant-velocity (CV) joints – these usually give few issues, but if the boots on the CV joints are neglected then these can become worn.

Clutch master cylinder

The clutch pedal is heavy compared to a modern car, but the clutch itself should engage smoothly. If not, it may be a sign of a failing master or slave cylinder. The master cylinder (if failing) will often leak into the cabin, therefore evidence of a past (or present) failure may be seen on the carpet. If the area indicated is wet

The clutch master cylinder can leak resulting in fluid leaking into the footwell and staining the carpet.

then replacement is due. The original fluid line between master and slave cylinder was a hard black plastic that could swell under pressure, particularly in hot weather. This should have been changed to a stainless steel flexible line.

Brakes

Does the car accelerate smoothly without pulling to one side or the other? Likewise, when applying the brakes, does the car stop without pulling harshly to one side or the other and without any undue noises? The brake calipers are pretty much standard late 1970s, with disc brakes all-round, and are cheap and easy to have refurbished. Often overlooked are the original rubber flexible brake lines, these should be updated to a modern stainless steel covered flexible line. How effective is the handbrake? This can seize and become ineffective from both lack of use and poor adjustment.

Final checks

Upon your return, allow the car to idle and again check for leaks both underneath the car and around the engine bay. If the A/C has been operating then you may see a small amount of clean water dripping from around the fuel tank cover plate area, usually closer to the passenger side. This is normal, and should just be the drain from the A/C plenum.

Evaluation procedure

Add up the total points. Score: 120 = excellent; 90 = good; 60 = average; 30 = poor. Cars scoring between 30 and 61 will require some serious work (at much the same cost regardless of score). Cars scoring between 62 and 83 will require very careful assessment of the necessary repair/restoration costs in order to arrive at a realistic value. Cars scoring over 84 will be completely usable, and will require only maintenance and care to preserve condition.

10 Auctions
– sold! Another way to buy your dream

Auction pros & cons

Pros: Prices will usually be similar to those of dealers or private sellers however you might grab a real bargain on the day. Auctioneers have usually established clear title with the seller. At the venue you can usually examine documentation relating to the vehicle.

Cons: You have to rely on a sketchy catalogue description of condition and history. The opportunity to inspect is limited, and you cannot drive the car. The Owners' Club may have some information on the car, so it's worth asking. Auction cars are often a little below par and may require some work. It's easy to overbid. There will usually be a buyer's premium to pay in addition to the auction hammer price.

Which auction?

Auctions by established auctioneers are advertised in car magazines and on the auction houses' websites. A catalogue, or a simple printed list of the lots for auctions might only be available a day or two ahead, though often lots are listed and pictured on auctioneers' websites much earlier. Contact the auction company to ask if previous auction selling prices are available, as this is useful information (details of past sales are often available on websites and in specialist classic car magazines).

Catalogue, entry fee and payment details

When you purchase the catalogue of the vehicles in the auction, it often acts as a ticket allowing two people to attend the viewing days and the auction. Catalogue details tend to be comparatively brief, but will include information such as 'one owner from new, low mileage, full service history,' etc. It will also usually show a guide price to give you some idea of what to expect to pay, and will tell you what is charged as a 'Buyer's premium.' The catalogue will also contain details of acceptable forms of payment. At the fall of the hammer an immediate deposit is usually required, the balance payable within 24 hours. If the plan is to pay by cash there may be a cash limit. Some auctions will accept payment by debit card. Sometimes credit or charge cards are acceptable, but will often incur an extra charge. A bank draft or bank transfer will have to be arranged in advance with your own bank, as well as with the auction house. No car will be released before **all** payments are cleared. If delays occur in payment transfers then storage costs can accrue.

Buyer's premium

A buyer's premium will be added to the hammer price: **don't** forget this in your calculations. It is not usual for there to be a further state tax or local tax on the purchase price and/or on the buyer's premium.

Viewing

In some instances it's possible to view on the day, or days before, as well as in the hours prior to, the auction. There are auction officials available who are willing to help out by opening engine and luggage compartments and to allow you to inspect the interior. While the officials may start the engine for you, a test drive is out of the question. Crawling under and around the car as much as you want is permitted, but you can't suggest that the car you are interested in be jacked up, or attempt to do the job yourself. You can also ask to see any documentation available.

Bidding

Before you take part in the auction, **decide your maximum bid – and stick to it!**

It may take a while for the auctioneer to reach the lot you are interested in, so use that time to observe how other bidders behave. When it's the turn of your car, attract the auctioneer's attention and make an early bid. The auctioneer will then look to you for a reaction every time another bid is made usually the bids will be in fixed increments until the bidding slows, when smaller increments will often be accepted before the hammer falls. If you want to withdraw from the bidding, make sure the auctioneer understands your intentions – a vigorous shake of the head when he or she looks to you for the next bid should do the trick!

Assuming that you are the successful bidder, the auctioneer will note your card or paddle number, and from that moment on you will be responsible for the vehicle.

If the car is unsold, either because it failed to reach the reserve or because there was little interest, it may be possible to negotiate with the owner, via the auctioneers, after the sale is over.

Successful bid

There are two more items to think about. How to get the car home, and insurance. If you can't drive the car, your own or a hired trailer is one way, another is to have the vehicle shipped using the facilities of a local company. The auction house will also have details of companies specialising in the transfer of cars. However please note that ideally DeLoreans should not be transported on an open trailer with the rear of the car facing in the direction of travel. It is not unknown for the air to get under the rear louvres and rip these off causing extensive damage to the car. If at all possible always tow/transport a DeLorean nose forward. This was the recommendation from the factory when the car was first produced and being shipped around the world. In reality, due to the weight bias of the car, if it is being transported on a trailer behind a car for example, then they are better transported with the rear to the front of the trailer. But please ensure that the louvres are very well strapped down and secured. Insurance for immediate cover can usually be purchased on site, but it may be more cost-effective to make arrangements with your own insurance company in advance, and then call to confirm the full details.

eBay & other online auctions could land you a car at a bargain price, though you'd be foolhardy to bid without examining the car first, something most vendors should encourage. A useful feature of eBay is that the geographical location of the car is shown, so you can narrow your choices to those within a realistic radius of home. Be prepared to be outbid in the last few moments of the auction. Remember, your bid is binding and that it will be very, very difficult to get restitution in the case of a crooked vendor fleecing you – **caveat emptor!**

Be aware that some cars offered for sale in online auctions are 'ghost' cars. **Don't** part with **any** cash without being sure that the vehicle does actually exist and is as described (usually pre-bidding inspection is possible). Genuine adverts will include details of the car's VIN, which you should be able to research via the Owners' Club. Since all DeLoreans look very similar, fraudulent sellers may try to substitute pictures of other cars. If in doubt ask for a photo with a specific item in the image, today's newspaper perhaps. A request for an image of a specific area or an area of the car not previously shown would be a good way to confirm that the car actually exists. There are many DeLorean specialists (particularly in the USA) who will check out any particular car and report on its condition for a fee.

Auctioneers

Barrett-Jackson www.barrett-jackson.com/ **Bonhams** www.bonhams.com/ **British Car Auctions BCA)** www.bca-europe.com or www.british-car-auctions.co.uk/ **Cheffins** www.cheffins.co.uk/ **Christies** www.christies.com/ **Coys** www.coys.co.uk/ **eBay** www.eBay.com/ **H&H** www.classic-auctions.co.uk/ **RM** www.rmauctions.com/ **Shannons** www.shannons.com.au/ **Silver** www.silverauctions.com

The superb rolling chassis restored by Lee Pattison on display at a DeLorean Owners' Club (UK) event.

11 Paperwork
– correct documentation is essential!

The paper trail
Classic, collector, and prestige cars usually come with a large portfolio of paperwork accumulated and passed on by a succession of proud owners. This documentation represents the real history of the car, and from it can be deduced the level of care the car has received, how much it's been used, which specialists have worked on it, and the dates of major repairs and restorations. All of this information will be priceless to you as the new owner, so be very wary of cars with little paperwork to support their claimed history. However, if the car is a recent import, as is often the case in the UK, it's not unusual to have little or no vehicle history.

Registration documents
All countries/states have some form of registration for private vehicles, whether it's like the American 'pink slip' system or the British 'log book' system.
   It is essential to check that the registration document is genuine, that it relates to the car in question, and that all the vehicle's details are correctly recorded, including chassis/VIN and engine numbers (if these are shown). Refer to chapter 5 for more details on DeLorean chassis/engine numbers, which are often missing or incorrect. If you are buying from the previous owner, his or her name and address should be recorded in the document: this will not be the case if you are buying from a dealer.
   In the UK the current (Euro-aligned) registration document is named "V5C," and is printed in coloured sections of blue, green and pink. The blue section relates to the car specification, the green section has details of the new owner and the pink section is sent to the DVLA in the UK when the car is sold. A small section in yellow deals with selling the car within the motor trade. The V5C must be obtained to tax the vehicle.

Previous ownership records
Due to the introduction of important new legislation on data protection, it is no longer possible to acquire, from the British DVLA, a list of previous owners of a car you own, or are intending to purchase. This also applies to dealerships and other specialists, who you may wish to acquire information from.
   If the car has a foreign registration there may be expensive and time-consuming formalities to complete, which vary around the world. None of these are too difficult to overcome, but research should be done to ascertain any regulations on importing a vehicle from one specific country to another. If the car is a recent import and has not been registered in the country you reside in, then check that all documentation to register the car is supplied and that any taxes/import duties have been paid and a receipt is provided. The DeLorean Owners' Club can provide any necessary documentation to aid with registering any DeLorean in the UK.

Roadworthiness certificate
Most country/state administrations require that vehicles are regularly tested to prove that they are safe to use on the public highway and do not produce excessive emissions. In the UK the MoT test is carried out at approved testing stations, for a fee. In the USA the requirement varies, but most states insist on an emissions test

every two years as a minimum, while the police are charged with pulling over unsafe looking vehicles.

In the UK the test is required on an annual basis, once a vehicle becomes three years old. Of particular relevance for older cars is that the certificate issued includes the mileage reading recorded at the test date and therefore becomes an independent record of that car's history. Ask the seller if previous certificates are available. Without an MoT the vehicle should be trailered to its new home, unless you insist that a valid MoT is part of the deal. (Not such a bad idea this, as at least you will know the car was roadworthy on the day it was tested. You don't need to wait for the old certificate to expire before having the test done.)

Road licence

The administration of every country/state charges some kind of tax for the use of its road system, the actual form of the 'road licence' and, how it is displayed, varying enormously country to country and state to state.

Whatever the form of the road licence, it must relate to the vehicle carrying it and must be present and valid if the car is to be driven on the public highway legally. The value of the licence will depend on the length of time it will continue to be valid.

Changed legislation in the UK means that the seller of a car must surrender any existing road fund licence, and it is the responsibility of the new owner to re-tax the vehicle at the time of purchase and before the car can be driven on the road. It's therefore vital to see the Vehicle Registration Certificate (V5C) at the time of purchase, and to have access to the New Keeper Supplement (V5C/2), allowing the buyer to obtain road tax immediately. If the car is untaxed because it has not been used for a period of time, the owner has to inform the licensing authorities, otherwise the vehicle's date-related registration number will be lost and there will be a painful amount of paperwork to get it re-registered.

Certificates of authenticity

For many makes of collectible car it is possible to get a certificate proving the age and authenticity (eg, engine and chassis numbers, paint colour and trim) of a particular vehicle, these are sometimes called 'Heritage Certificates' these are however, impossible to obtain for a DeLorean car.

The DeLorean museum (www.deloreanmuseum.org) may be able to supply (for a fee) a reproduction window sticker that was attached to the car prior to shipment to the dealer. Also available for certain cars is an 'original owner information' certificate, and a copy of the original warranty certificate. These give details (where available) on the original selling dealer/sale date and first owner. For UK registration, the Owners' Club can supply a dating certificate that is acceptable for the DVLA to register any imported DeLorean car in the UK.

If the car has been used in European classic car rallies it may have a FIVA (Fédération Internationale des Véhicules Anciens) certificate. The so-called 'FIVA

The window sticker that would have originally been fitted to the car prior to sale in the USA. Reproductions are available from the DeLorean museum.

Passport,' or 'FIVA Vehicle Identity Card,' enables organisers and participants to recognise whether or not a particular vehicle is suitable for individual events. If you want to obtain such a certificate, go to www.fbhvc.co.uk or www.fiva.org. There will be similar organisations in other countries too.

Valuation certificate

Hopefully, the vendor will have a recent valuation certificate, or letter signed by a recognised expert stating how much he, or she, believes the particular car to be worth (such documents, together with photos, are usually needed to get 'agreed value' insurance). Generally such documents should act only as confirmation of your own assessment of the car, rather than a guarantee of value, as the expert has probably not seen the car in the flesh. The easiest way to find out how to obtain a formal valuation for insurance purposes is to contact the Owners' Club.

Above: a 1981 DeLorean instruction manual and plastic wallet. Right: the 1981 car maintenance and instruction booklets.

Service history

Often these cars will have been serviced at home by enthusiastic (and hopefully capable) owners for many years. Nevertheless, try to obtain as much service history/ invoices and other paperwork pertaining to the car as you can. Specialist garage receipts score most points in the value stakes. However, anything helps in the great authenticity game, items like the original bill of sale, handbook, parts invoices and repair bills, adding to the story and the character of the car. Even a brochure correct to the year of the car's manufacture is a useful document and something that you could well have to search hard to locate in future years. If the seller claims that the car has been restored, then expect receipts and other evidence from a specialist restorer.

If the seller claims to have carried out regular servicing, ask what work was completed, when, and seek some evidence of it being carried out. Your assessment of the car's overall condition should tell you whether the seller's claims are genuine.

Restoration photographs

If the seller tells you that the car has been restored, then expect to be shown a series of photographs taken while the restoration was under way. Pictures taken at various stages, and from various angles, should help you gauge the thoroughness of the work. If you buy the car, ask if you can have all the photographs, as they form an important part of the vehicle's history. It's surprising how many sellers are happy to part with their car and accept your cash, but want to hang on to their photographs! In the latter event, you may be able to persuade the vendor to get a set of copies made.

Original sales and publicity brochures.

12 What's it worth?
– let your head rule your heart

Condition

If the car you've been looking at is in really bad condition, or a restoration project, then you've probably not bothered to use the marking system in chapter 9 – the 60 minute evaluation. You may not have even got as far as using that chapter at all!

If you did use the marking system in chapter 9 you'll know whether the car is in Excellent (maybe Concours), Good, Average or Poor condition or, perhaps, somewhere in-between these categories.

Many classic/collector car magazines run a regular price guide. If you haven't bought the latest editions, do so now and compare their suggested values for the model you are thinking of buying: also look at the auction prices they're reporting. And don't forget, owners' clubs are a great place to start for pre-purchase advice. Trends can change too. The values published in the magazines tend to vary from one magazine to another, as do their scales of condition, so read carefully the guidance notes they provide. Bear in mind that a car that is truly a recent show winner could be worth more than the highest scale published. Assuming that the car you have in mind is not in show/concours condition, then relate the level of condition that you judge the car to be in with the appropriate guide price. How does the figure compare with the asking price? Before you start haggling with the seller, consider what effect any variation from standard specification might have on the car's value. A painted DeLorean, for example, will always be worth less than a bare stainless steel car, please see chapter 14 for more information on painted DeLoreans. Remember if you are buying from a dealer, there will be a dealer's premium in the price.

Desirable options/extras

Luggage rack, side stripes or an upgraded stereo system may or may not be something on your wish list. Factory options were limited to a luggage rack with optional ski rack adaptor, a thin grey side stripe with DMC logo, a wide black stripe that sat usually below the 'rubbing' strips, floor mats, cleaning kits and a car cover.

Certain electrical upgrades such as modern cooling fans or automatic door openers may also be something that you require. Many vendors do have

A car with the thin grey stripe and DMC logo.

modern and updated fuel/suspension/braking and engine upgrade (stage 1/2/3) packages, that may or may not be something that you desire. Where upgraded parts have been fitted it's always worth asking if the vendor still has the original component (and possibly any spare parts they have accumulated) and then perhaps negotiating for them to be included in the price. Some parts can be difficult or expensive to obtain and you may wish to revert the car back to 'stock' at a later date.

The large black side stripe on an early car with dark grey wheels. (Courtesy Claire Wright)

Original black carpet mats.

Undesirable features

Non-stock engine, non-stock interiors, upgraded stereo system depending on your preference, badly botched electrical systems, or aftermarket wheels.

Striking a deal

Negotiate on the basis of your condition assessment, mileage, and fault rectification cost. Also take into account the car's specification. Be realistic about the value but don't be completely intractable: a small compromise on the part of the vendor or buyer will often facilitate a deal at little real cost.

An original car cleaning set and its contents.

13 Do you really want to restore?
– it'll take longer and cost more than you think

The important questions are, how much restoration work are you willing to take on, and who is going to do the work? Some people are more than capable of doing extensive mechanical/chassis work, but are unable to do bodywork and trim, though, with a DeLorean, the stainless steel bodywork is in itself a specialist material that few have the skills to repair to 'as new' condition.

We are fortunate in the UK to have the incredibly skilled Chris Nicholson, who is a master of all things stainless, but depending on the condition of the stainless, costs can soon escalate, particularly if there is accident damage. The body is surprisingly easy to separate from the chassis, being held on by just ten bolts. This is easily done by one person, and, as the cars are aging, this is becoming a more common occurrence due to past neglect. The frame can then either be repaired or even replaced with a new stainless steel item. Restoration is reasonably easy, due to the frame being originally made of mild steel. Removing the epoxy coating is more of a challenge, and is often done by acid dipping to remove the epoxy from the box sections. The frame can then, after repairs, be galvanised

The body tub complete with all its panels is surprisingly easy to separate from the chassis, allowing a full refurbishment to take place.

Left: a frame showing some corrosion. In this case the damage was fairly localised, and the repair was simple after the frame had been stripped of its epoxy coating. Above: the same frame having been stripped of epoxy, localised repairs carried out and 'E-coated.'

and powder-coated or E-coated (electrophoretic coating) to protect it for many years to come. Replating and refurbishing all parts to an as-new condition can also be carried out at this point, prior to covering it all back up with the body. The biggest cost in any restoration is always labour, and will far outweigh the cost of a good car, so, before buying a complete wreck, be realistic about whether you can actually do the work yourself.

A heavily corroded front frame would need extensive work if not a complete new frame. (Courtesy Alex Manos, Beverly Hills Car Club)

The bodytub is a similar material to GRP, and can be repaired by any skilled individual who has the experience of working on glass-fibre, but again these repairs can prove costly and time-consuming to repair correctly. If it is an accident-damaged car it will be hard to lose the 'stigma' attached to this, especially within such a small community of owners, and subsequent value may be affected.

The drivetrain and mechanical systems are fairly robust, but as a project car it will be difficult to fully assess the condition. Before attempting to start the vehicle, please read chapter 15 regarding lack of use – particularly the section regarding the fuel system.

The engine and gearbox can be easily extracted, assisted by the fact that all of the rear sections of the car can be removed for better access.

Interiors can suffer from spending decades in the hot US sunshine, causing the complete interior to be sun-baked. Some items, such as the dashboards, have been reproduced, but most of the rest of the interior trim can be re-trimmed by a professional vehicle trimmer. Seat covers are available as modern replacements from vendors, and some supplies of NOS (new old stock) are still available in limited quantities. However, the costs of a full re-trim can soon add up, as most of the work is usually beyond even the most competent home enthusiast.

Left: a typical sight upon entering the VOD for the first time, if it has never been cleaned out.

Right: cylinder head removed showing the piston liners, with extensive build-up of corrosion and debris.

14 Paint problems
– bad complexion, including dimples, pimples and bubbles

No DeLorean left the factory as a painted car, in fact there was not even a paint shop at the factory. Many DeLoreans now exist in painted colours, and can, and do, look really good. Three of them were reputedly painted upon instruction from DMCL upon arrival in the USA. Some were painted by the selling dealer when new, to try and increase sales, some at the request of owners and some to hide accident damage. Any painted DeLorean is worth less than an original stainless steel car. The following points

A purple painted car in the US, an unusual colour choice but works well. (Courtesy Mike Hooper)

apply only to a painted DeLorean, and are similar to that of any mild steel painted car, with the exception that it is not unusual for the existing perfect panels to have been 'roughed up' in an attempt to provide a 'key' for the paint on the panels. However, clearly, there should be no rust hiding beneath the paintwork!

Paint faults generally occur due to lack of protection/maintenance or to poor preparation prior to a respray or touch-up. Some of the following conditions may be present in a painted car you're looking at.

Orange peel
This appears as an uneven paint surface, similar to the appearance of the skin of an orange. The fault is caused by the failure of atomized paint droplets to flow into each other when they hit the surface. It's sometimes possible to rub out the effect with proprietary paint cutting/rubbing compound or very fine grades of abrasive paper. A respray may be necessary in severe cases. Consult a bodywork repairer/paint shop for advice on the particular car.

Cracking
Severe cases are likely to have been caused by too heavy an application of paint (or filler beneath the paint). Also, insufficient stirring of the paint before application can lead to the components being improperly mixed, and cracking can result. Incompatibility with the paint already on the panel can have a similar effect. To rectify the problem it is necessary to rub down to a smooth, sound finish before respraying the problem area.

A red-painted car at one of the Owners' Club meetings.

Black really suits a DeLorean, and is a common colour seen on a painted car.
(Courtesy Mike Hooper)

This can also occur on the front and rear facia of a DeLorean where they have been re-painted/refinished.

Crazing
Sometimes the paint takes on a crazed rather than a cracked appearance when the problems mentioned under 'Cracking' are present. This problem can also be caused by a reaction between the underlying surface and the paint. Paint removal and respraying the problem area is usually the only solution. Again this can also occur on the flexible front and rear facia from minor impact damage and poor refinishing/painting.

Micro blistering & blistering
Usually the result of an economy respray where inadequate heating has allowed moisture to settle on the car before spraying. Consult a paint specialist, but usually damaged paint will have to be removed before partial or full respraying. Can also be caused by car covers that don't 'breathe'.

Fading
Some colours, especially reds, are prone to fading if subjected to strong sunlight for long periods without the benefit of polish protection. Sometimes proprietary paint restorers and/or paint cutting/rubbing compounds will retrieve the situation. Often a respray is the only real solution.

Peeling
Often a problem with metallic paintwork when the sealing lacquer becomes

damaged and begins to peel off. Poorly applied paint may also peel. The remedy is to strip and start again! This can also occur where poor preparation of the stainless has allowed the paint not to adhere properly. Peeling can also appear on the front and rear facias of a DeLorean if badly repainted.

Dimples
Dimples in the paintwork are caused by the residue of polish (particularly silicone types) not being removed properly before respraying. Paint removal and repainting is the only solution.

Dents
If the car is already painted then depending on your long-term plans for the car (you may wish to remove the paint in the future) then the dent can be filled and the panel can be repainted. However, do ensure that no further damage is done to the area/panel in order to facilitate this.

Restoring a painted DeLorean back to stainless steel
This has been done many times, with varying degrees of success. The quality of the end result is usually dictated by the condition of the stainless steel below the paint. If badly damaged in many areas then it may be better to leave the car painted, as the costs of restoration are likely to far outweigh the cost of a non-painted car. The paint can be removed by paint stripper, and soda blasting has also proved to work well. After the paint has been removed, the car will still need to be fully re-brushed to restore the graining effect in the stainless steel necessary to match the original factory finish. Unless you have the skills and confidence to do this, then a non-painted car may be better for you.

Remember, working with stainless steel is a unique skill. Unlike on a painted car, mishaps can't be corrected by touch-up paints or a visit to your local body shop. In fact, even cleaning the stainless steel properly will be a new experience – 'along the grain' is the method, whereas circular 'wax on, wax off' motions are to be avoided. That said, the stainless steel can also be very forgiving. Tree sap, road tar, and other similar mishaps can be removed without fear of damage to any paint.

Another-red painted car. Note this example is also fitted with the optional luggage rack. (Courtesy Mike Hooper)

15 Problems due to lack of use
– just like their owners, DeLoreans need exercise

Cars, like humans, are at their most efficient if they exercise regularly. A run of at least ten miles, once a week, is recommended for classics. DeLoreans, in particular, do not like lack of use. Unfortunately, being a car that is often purchased by long-term collectors and museums, this only makes the issue more prevalent.

Seized components
Depending on the amount of time the car has been standing (often for long periods in the case of a DeLorean) then you should check if the engine itself turns freely, prior to attempting to start it on the starter motor. Pistons in brake calipers, slave and master cylinders can seize and leak. Depending on the length of time the vehicle has stood, all of the hydraulics may have to be completely rebuilt or replaced. The clutch may seize if the plate becomes stuck to the flywheel because of corrosion, and handbrakes (parking brakes) can seize if the cables and linkages rust.

The location of the clutch and brake master cylinder. The clutch master cylinder has its own reservoir that can leak, causing extensive damage to the epoxy on the frame below. The red pipe is a stainless steel braided clutch line going to the slave cylinder.

Clutch master cylinder
Brake master cylinder

Fluids
Old, acidic oil can corrode bearings. Uninhibited coolant can corrode internal waterways. Lack of antifreeze can cause core plugs to be pushed out, even cracks in the block or head. Silt settling and solidifying can cause overheating. Water pumps also are prone to failure after having been sat for some time. Brake fluid absorbs water from the atmosphere and should be renewed every two years, though this is often overlooked.

Tyre problems
Tyres that have had the weight of the car on them in a single position for some time will develop flat spots, resulting in some (usually temporary) vibration. The tyre walls may have cracks or (blister-type)

The 'Y' pipe that's normally hidden by the water pump and intake manifold has become completely clogged with congealed old antifreeze. The removed water pump and engine block were all in a similar condition.

bulges, meaning new tyres are needed. Many DeLoreans coming out of storage still have the original tyres that they left the factory with, these being Goodyear NCT HR600. Clearly no one should be driving around on 35-year-old rubber. Shock absorbers (dampers) with lack of use will lose their elasticity or even seize. Creaking, groaning and stiff suspension are signs of this problem.

Rubber and plastic
Radiator hoses may have perished and split, possibly resulting in the loss of all coolant. Window and door seals can harden and leak. Rubber gaiters and boots can crack. Wiper blades will harden.

Electrics
The battery will be of little use if it has not been charged for many months. Earthing/grounding problems are common when the connections have corroded. Old bullet and spade type electrical connectors commonly rust/corrode, and will need disconnecting, cleaning and protection (eg, dielectric grease). Sparkplug electrodes will often have corroded in an unused engine. Wiring insulation can harden and fail.

Fuel system
Whilst the Bosch K-Jetronic (K-Jet) system works efficiently when maintained, it is one of the DeLorean's main issues, as it does not take well to neglect and lack of use. Unleaded fuel, in particular, degrades over time (in as little as six months), and left over many years, as often these cars are, then problems with the K-Jet system can occur. The very worst thing that can happen to any DeLorean that has been in storage or simply not used for a few years, is to just pour new fuel in the tank and attempt to start it. The old fuel must be drained, and the tank must be thoroughly cleaned out (or replaced) and inspected before even putting a battery on the vehicle. It may be found that many of the components within the tank have simply rotted away (especially rubber components). First, clean and replace as many of the fuel components within the fuel tank as are required, only then should you introduce clean new fuel. Then move on to changing filters and flushing out all fuel lines, and cleaning as many other components as possible with clean fuel, prior to even attempting to start the vehicle. Further advice and guidance on this process can be obtained from the Owners' Club, and many of the DeLorean online forums around the world.

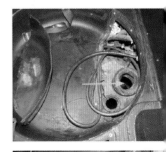

Top right: the fuel tank with the access cover removed. Note the fuel pump support sealing ring (arrowed) has disintegrated. The hole below is for the tank sender unit which is also missing. All the access covers are secured by machine screws into 'rivet nuts' mounted into the body tub, these can corrode stripping the 'rivet nut' out of the tub. Bottom right: a refurbished VOD (Valley of Death) with new water pump and hoses fitted showing the location of the 'Y' pipe.

Clubs

The UK DeLorean Owners' Club (www.deloreans.co.uk) has been established for over 25 years, founded by the honorary club president Dave Howarth and Simon Lees-Milne. The club has gone from strength to strength, publishing a quarterly full-colour A4 magazine, that is shipped to its worldwide membership base, as well as exhibiting at major car shows in the UK and organising club meets. The club has helped to develop new/modern replacement parts, and a small selection is supplied through the club's shop. The club is a member of the FBHVC, and recognised by the DVLA for verification of a car's build date.

Over 30 years of motoring history.

The DeLorean Owners Club UK
www.deloreans.co.uk

The DeLorean Owners Association (www.deloreanowners.org) is the American based club with 'chapters' across the US and Ireland. They also organise events including the very successful 'Eurofest' gathering every four years in Belfast, as well as many other US-based events. The 'Eurofest' is almost a pilgrimage for any new owner, as it normally includes a visit and tour to the original DeLorean factory and test track at Dunmurry.

There are many local clubs within Europe, and throughout America and Canada. A quick internet search for a DeLorean club in your country or locality would be the best way to find other owners close to you.

There are also countless DeLorean specialist forums throughout the world (eg UK Owners' Club: www.deloreans.co.uk/forum), who form a superb knowledge base, and are full of very supportive and experienced enthusiasts who have had the same problems and issues that you may have.

DeLoreans and owners/club members preparing for an indoor show in the UK.

Approximately 60 DeLoreans congregate in front of the parliament building at Stormont, Northern Ireland, as part of the 2016 Eurofest gathering.

Parts suppliers & specialists

UK
www.deloreans.co.uk
www.deloreango.com
www.pjgrady.co.uk
www.delorean.co.uk

Non-UK
www.delorean.com
www.delorean.eu
www.pjgrady.com
www.deloreanindustries.com
www.deloreanautoparts.com
www.delorean-parts.com

Books

There have been many books published over the years about the DeLorean car and JZ DeLorean himself. Some are very good. Some, particularly the ones written many years ago, are factually inaccurate, but still worthy of a read. These are probably four of the best, in my opinion:

DeLorean – Celebrating the Impossible, by Chris Parnham and Andrew Withers. ISBN 978-0992859404
John Z, the DeLorean and Me … tales from an insider, by Barrie Wills. ISBN 978-0985657888
The DeLorean Story: The Car, The People, The Scandal, by Nick Sutton. ISBN 978-0857333148
DeLorean: Stainless Steel Illusion, by John Lamm. ISBN: 978-0974414102

Other useful books:

The factory-published *Workshop Manual*, *Technical Information Manual*, and *Parts Manual* are all worthy of purchase from the main DeLorean vendors.
Haynes Manual *Volvo 260*, book number 400 (engine section applicable).

DeLoreans going around the factory test track in Dunmurry, Belfast. (Courtesy Harry Woolliams)

17 Vital statistics
– essential data at your fingertips

The following statistics were all taken from the original DMC manuals

Engine data
All alloy with a single overhead camshaft per cylinder head, with 'wet' renewable cast iron cylinder liners and all alloy pistons.
Number of cylinders: 6, 'V' formation
Bore: 91mm
Stroke: 73mm
Engine capacity: 2849cc
Compression ratio: 8.8:1
Maximum power: 130bhp
Maximum torque: 208nm
Must use unleaded fuel, as factory fitted with catalytic converter.

Cooling system
Positive pressure closed system, water/ethylene glycol, with radiator mounted at the front of the car with twin thermostatically controlled fans.

Fuel system
Bosch K-Jetronic continuous mechanical fuel-injection system, with electric pump situated in the fuel tank. Has an in-tank mounted gauze filter and a frame mounted fuel filter.

Ignition system
Bosch electronic contactless distributor, firing order: 1-6-3-5-2-4

Suspension
Lotus designed, the front having unequal length upper and lower control arms with coil springs, Girling telescopic shock absorber with stabiliser bar. Rear: diagonal trailing arms (adjustable via the Trailing Arm Bolt) with upper and lower (non adjustable) link arms. Coil springs fitted over Girling telescopic shock absorbers.

Wheels
Cast light alloy
    Front: 14in x 6in fitted with 195/60 HR14 tyres
    Rear: 15in x 8in fitted with 235/60 HT15 tyres
    Spare: 15in x 4in fitted with T125/70 D15 tyre

Steering
Rack and pinion with adjustable collapsible column.
Turning circle: 43ft (13.1m)
Steering wheel turns, lock-to-lock: 2.4

Braking system
Front and rear power-assisted non-vented discs, front 254mm, rear 275mm, mechanical self-adjusting parking brake to rear discs.

Chassis/body
Epoxy coated mild steel backbone chassis (Lotus designed) with a reinforced glass fibre underbody clad in grade 304 stainless steel body panels.

Capacities and dimensions
Overall length: 166in (4213mm
Overall width: 73.10in (1856mm)
Height: (doors closed) 44.90in (1140mm)
Height: (doors open) 77.20in (1962mm)
Ground clearance (OE spec): front: 5.60in (142mm); rear: 6.10in (155mm)
Weight: approximately 2716lb (1233kg) (varies depending on transmission type and fuel level)
Fuel capacity: 11.3 gallons (51.5 litres)
Weight distribution: 35% front/65% rear

Notes
The DMC-12 features heavy doors that are opened via the use of cryogenically preset torsion bars and gas-charged struts. The torsion bars were developed by Grumman Aerospace to withstand the stresses of supporting the doors. A popular misconception of the DMC-12's gull-wing doors is that they require far more side clearance to open than an ordinary side hinged door. In fact the opposite is true, the doors only require a clearance of 11 inches (28cm) to fully open, making the opening and closing of the doors in crowded spaces or garages far easier than most cars. The body was designed by Giorgetto Giugiaro of ItalDesign.

Back To The Future
It's hard not to bring up the *Back To The Future* film franchise and its continuing influence on the DMC-12. Throughout this book I have tried not to include many references to *BTTF* simply because this book is designed to be a buyer's guide and not a history on the DeLorean car. However there is no denying that the film franchise has helped to ensure the enduring popularity of the DMC-12, bringing the appeal of the car to a new audience and ensuring that the timeless design of the DeLorean lives on to a new and younger audience.

Abbreviations
A/C   Air-conditioning
ASI   Audio Systems Incorporated
BAE   British Aerospace Engineering
BTTF   *Back To The Future*
CV   Constant velocity (joint)
DMC   DeLorean Motor Cars
DMCL   DeLorean Motor Cars Ltd
DMCH   DeLorean Motor Company Houston
DOC   DeLorean Owners' Club (UK)
DVLA   Driver and Vehicle Licensing Agency

ECU	Electronic control unit
ERM	Elastic reservoir moulding
FBHVC	Federation of British Historic Vehicle Clubs
FFE	Front frame extension
GKN	Guest, Keen & Nettlefolds, automotive and aerospace company
GRP	Glass reinforced plastic
IHI	Japanese turbo manufacturer
JZD	John Zachary DeLorean
K-Jet	Bosch K-Jetronic continuous mechanical fuel-injection system
LCA	Lower control arm
LED	Light emitting diode
LHD	Left-hand drive
NOS	New old stock (unused original part)
OE	Original equipment
PRV	Peugeot-Renault-Volvo
RHD	Right-hand drive
TAB	Trailing arm bolt
UAE	United Arab Emirates
VARI	Vacuum assisted resin injection
VIN	Vehicle identification number
VOD	Valley of death – the 'V' area at the centre of the engine block

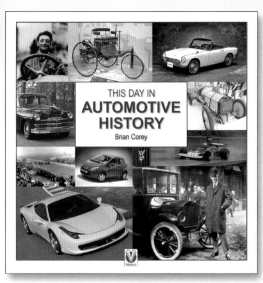

... don't buy a vehicle until you've read one of these!

Index